Crossroads

Crossroads

Jude Addo

To order additional copies of this book, contact:
Xlibris Corporation
0-800-644-6988
www.xlibrispublishing.co.uk
Orders@xlibrispublishing.co.uk
304382

Contents

Praise for Crossroads

Absolutely wonderful! Crossroads presents a personal testimony of success in the secular world fostered by the pursuit of spiritual purpose. It explains, by way of mundane experiences, some of the essential teachings of the Bible. It's clear descriptions are just beautiful to behold; it's simple but poignant teachings and analogies are enthralling, making each page a pleasure to peruse.

The especially jovial style of the book gives you a bitter-sweet feeling, where the author's jokes keep you laughing, and yet his more serious revelations about the Christian's excellence make you want to cry for not doing more than you are capable of. Indeed, this is a cocktail of spirit and soul in book form. An amazing read and must-have. I dare you to put it down for five minutes.

FRANCIS N. AGYIN-ASARE
Author, *Upon Delilah's Knees*

*   *   *   *

I found myself laughing one moment and then deeply moved and challenged the next. Jude does a great job at painting the picture of an everyday young man, and by the same token, he exemplifies the exuberance of a Spirit led life. This book is both refreshing and thought provoking.

For those who feel the longing for more in life, I believe that this book will help to feed the eternal cravings that all humans have for identity, purpose and destiny. There is more to life, and Jude helps us through this journey to seek and find the God that created us and put eternity in our hearts.

MARCO DEBARROS
Young Adults Pastor, *New Life Worship Center*

* * * *

This book takes us on a remarkable journey that encapsulates the life-changing testimony of a man touched by God. Every stroke of ink brilliantly paints a vivid image of who God wants us to be, how to get there, and unequivocally addresses the detrimental, stereotypical schools of thought prevailing in our society.

The clever blend of humor and severity makes Crossroads such a pleasure to read. Jude's words are spiritually challenging, intellectually stimulating and yet heartwarming. This book is truly a revelation that is clear, concise and unbelievably striking.

ALPHONSE ASARE
Founder, *Fellowship of the Unashamed (Bryant University)*

* * * *

Crossroads is an exciting and life changing book—it is equally thought provoking and an amazing piece of work.

Jude has used his personal life experiences to direct you to the source of all creation and to mankind's dominion and authority over all things. He opens your eyes to the challenges that are common to the human race but in that same breath directs you to the way of overcoming the same.

This book will help you to re-evaluate your current position and begin to search for the purpose for which you were created. I am confident, without a shadow of a doubt, that at the end of your reading you will know what to do to move to the next level (your place of authority and right standing) and attain your purpose in life.

LADY GIFTY TETTEH
Barrister, *Chambers of G D Tetteh*

Foreword

Crossroads—*definition: a crucial point, a crisis situation or point in time when a critical decision must be made; A road that crosses another.*

Isaiah 30:21—Your ears will hear a word behind you, "This is the way, walk in it," whenever you turn to the right or to the left.

You are holding in your hands a book that recounts the captivating story of an incredible transformation and the evidence of the manifold Grace of God in a man who dared to follow the prompting of God to write.

From the mandate to "write that book" to this finished product, Jude Addo has managed to put fresh paint on old and battered signposts often ignored in the pilgrimage of life's journey.

Jeremiah 6:16—Thus says the LORD, "Stand by the ways and see and ask for the ancient paths, where the good way is, and walk in it; And you will find rest for your souls. But they said, 'We will not walk in it.'

With eye opening insights unusual in one who has only travelled "the path" in four short years, and his reflection upon the providence and steering hand of God, Jude has picked up the pen of the ready-writer, and successfully conveyed in easy to read style, weathered themes often overlooked in this fast paced, multi-choice, alternative lifestyle obsessed times, that refocuses and centers on a tried, tested and proven roadmap to finding true rest and purpose for the muddled traveler.

Crossroads is a book that is difficult to put down. The lure of this book is the urge to keep reading through due to its ability to connect with, and compel the reader to look at their journey with fresh perspectives on life transforming truths.

I have personally read through Crossroads three times and so far, from his testimony to nuggets on the drive of purpose, the release of power through understanding the principle of sacrifice, to the life-impacting creative reality of words, from the rationality of faith to disabusing of the mind of wrong concepts of Holiness, I have not ceased to be refreshed in some context by the simple sincerity and transparency of thoughts behind these words.

After over 50 years and countless "crossroads" moments in my life and ministry, Jude's timely book is a stirring reminder and a source of inspiration to hold on to the 'good way' that leads to rest for the wearied soul.

Bishop Dick Essandoh
Action Chapel U.K & Europe

Preface

It would probably come to you as no surprise if I told you that I am not a best-selling author. I have neither coauthored a book nor been involved in the authorship of one. In fact, this book you hold in your hand signifies my very first attempt at book writing. Brace yourselves.

One toxic trait that I carried from my infancy to my teenage years was my pervasive disinterest in reading. I had been gifted many books over the years, all of which collected dust. If you were gracious enough to hand me a book with pictures, I would carefully examine the images and their corresponding captions and amiably consider the book read. Reading was a nightmare. Some may find it ironic then, how I decided to write a book—you're not alone, I too find it ironic. So why did I resolve to write this book? Beats me. In all honesty, I cannot assert that I genuinely had a desire to write one.

In my bathroom one spring morning I heard a voice in my heart instructing me to put my pen to paper and start writing a book. This was no strange voice, but I immediately dismissed it for the reasons above—inexperience in authoring and my childhood disinterest in reading. Moreover, I had neither the tools nor resources to get published. I was convicted that these were secondary issues, but fear gripped my heart so tight that it clouded my judgment.

A couple of days later, I was invited to attend a Prayer Summit hosted by Action Chapel International where a man with a prophetic gift was leading the church in prayer. I was eager to hear a word from this prophet concerning my life. I left the conference disappointed . . . but not for long. As a friend and I stood on the platform awaiting the eastbound Central Line, we were approached by a young man who mentioned that he was also in attendance at the Prayer Summit. This man had such a strong positive bias towards the prophetic gift that it led me to believe that indeed he considered himself to be part of that ministerial office. A few minutes into the conversation he began telling me things about my life that were shockingly accurate, and closed with this remark: "you must write that book". Utterly astounded, I asked him how he knew about the book (a very daft question to ask a prophet you would think).

This left a bitter-sweet taste in my mouth. Although it appeared the conviction in my heart had been confirmed, I was still unsure as to whether I had the bravado to write a single word under the designation of an author. As humbling as this mandate was, I remembered that obedience is better than sacrifice at all times and in all seasons of life.

In this book I reveal a great deal about my life that I can envisage many will find an element of satire in. Albeit somewhat unintentional, the purpose is to make the book as easy a read as possible; if you're anything like me, reading convoluted books can be a daunting experience. Nonetheless, I solemnly beseech you not to acquire a taste for satire so strong that you permit it to be a distraction from the main crux of this account. I strongly believe that there is a timeless message herein that will be an immense blessing to your life.

A final caveat: this book is not a purely Christian book nor is it a secular book. I believe divorcing man's spiritual life from his secular life blurs the manifestation of God's blessing in any presentation. My prayer is that the sharing of my life, struggles, and insight into the things of God revealed through this book, will benefit you in ways that cannot be readily achieved through a personal interaction. Please take the time to read the words of this book carefully. Be blessed!

All scriptures presented in this book are taken out of the New American Standard Bible (NASB) version unless otherwise stated.

Dedication

This book is dedicated to my father, Commander James Kwabena Addo.

Acknowledgements

It wouldn't be Christian of me if I didn't give all praise and gratitude first and foremost to the Lord Jesus Christ who loved this rascal enough to pay my ransom. I owe Him my all and give Him the entire honor.

Thank you to my parents and especially to a prayerful mother who petitioned to God on countless occasions for her wayward son. Without the sacrifices you made and sweat you bore on my behalf, I would not be who I am today. I would also like to show gratitude to my family for their support and encouragement through my years in university and efforts in ministry.

Thanks to Alphonse, a man I consider my father and friend in ministry. Thank you for training, encouraging, and rebuking me where I needed correction. I owe much to you.

Thank you to Bishop Dag Heward-Mills. Your books have been a huge blessing to me and have increased my knowledge, appreciation, and understanding of the things of God.

Many thanks to Bishop Dick Essandoh of Action Chapel International. I truly appreciate your help, guidance, and exhortation.

Many thanks go to a wonderful friend, Annabel. I am grateful to you for your unconditional support, love, and the genuineness of your friendship. God richly bless you for your efforts!

Thanks to the Fellowship of the Unashamed (F.O.T.U) for their loyalty and dedication to the preaching of the gospel. Your efforts are not in vain.

Thanks to Nana Frema and the entire Team Jesus group for giving me the opportunity to speak at the conference in Ghana. Your efforts and dedication in seeing people reconciled to God will be remembered always.

Thank you to Francis Agyin-Asare for sharing your invaluable insight into the world of publishing and for being a source of encouragement. It is much appreciated.

I am grateful to Pastor Marco of New Life Worship Center. Thank you for mentoring me in seasons where I needed it most. I appreciate all the guidance I have received from you.

Finally, thanks to all friends and supporters who have been so kind as to patronize this book. I thank you for the confidence you have placed in me. I pray this book will be as much a blessing to you as it has been to me. Thank you loads.

Chapter 1

MY TESTIMONY

I believe it would be disingenuous of me to present to you the Gospel without giving you the lens through which it is seen. This chapter serves to disclose personal aspects of my life in order for you to fully grasp the perspective from which the things of God are expressed.

Early Years

I am the last born in a family of twelve. And no, my mother did not give birth to twelve children—that would be stupendous. Both parents were in previous marriages and at some point in history came together to have five children, of which I was the baby. I am not a man of noble birth, neither was my father. In fact, during my father's tenure as a politician he was forced into voluntary exile in the Ivory Coast due to a series of violent upheavals in our native country, Ghana.

I wouldn't dare to say that I was a fatherless child in my infant years due to this. It seems that most successful men today reinforce their tireless appetite for success in the minds of their supporters by constantly indicating that their father was not around. As if to subtly boast "Yeah, I did it without a father, I'm the man!" I didn't do anything without a father. Who am I kidding; I have not even achieved anything significant enough to utter those words. Regardless, I had a mother who played the role of mummy and daddy in the absence of my father. This woman was tough I tell you! Mom, if you're reading this let me use this opportunity to inform you, with respect, that you had the fist of a man!

My father was given permission to return to Ghana when I was six years old. Even in his absence this man provided for his family remotely, sending us to private school and making provision for our daily needs. I can't even complain about his exile, it gave me a free holiday every vacation period. Whilst other kids were off to Europe and the Americas, I could boast that I took a ten hour road trip to Abidjan—fun. Excusing the levity, I truly believe my father's absence was more of a blessing than a curse due to the impact it had on my mother.

Mother became a Jesus freak during these years. Her husband was away, who else could she put her trust in? She did have the fist of a man but developed the heart of an angel. She was incredibly churchy and encouraged all of her children to embrace faith and become prayerful. I wasn't buying it though, which probably has something to do with the fact that I was only three years old. But even as the years elapsed and with my father present, I became increasingly rebellious—smoking, drinking, womanizing, and living for the day.

During my years in high school, for one reason or another I became a little wiser in my ways, which I can guarantee you had nothing to do with my relationship with God, or lack thereof. At this time, my mother decided to conveniently disclose to me a dream she had before I was born. She was desperate for another boy—after having five girls, I don't blame her. In her dream, she was told she would conceive a boy, and the boy would be a man of God who would bring joy to her household. Now, in no way do I reveal this to you as a boast or connotation to consider myself a special child. In fact, those who truly know me would agree that I am a person who relentlessly dislikes attention. I try to avoid attention at all costs to the extent that I actually do not stand up in a plane even if I desperately need to use the washroom. Personally, I simply do not like eyes on me.

My mother's revelation of this child she was about to bear was kept a secret until my years in high school. I found the thought of being a 'man of God' bizarre as a relationship with God was nonexistent. To be precise, I never went to church. On days I miraculously found myself at church, my cousin and I would escape during the break to a friend's house up the street to play video games (Mother, I'm sorry you had to find out this way). Admittedly, when I was actually eager to attend church, it was by virtue of the fact that I wanted a taste of the meat pie sold at the entrance of the church building. I had no concept of who God was, and it certainly confused me whenever the name of Jesus was mentioned. If church was about God, why did we so often spend half the service talking about Jesus? These questions never bothered me enough to find out more. I was content in my ignorance.

The Trial

A few years later I was enrolled at Bryant University in Rhode Island, studying Economics. Four years in college was the perfect opportunity to be idiotic to my heart's content and I made sure I was going to make the most of it. Coincidentally, I was enrolled in the same university as a friend from high school, Alphonse. Now Alphonse was certainly not your typical knucklehead. He did have a relationship with God, perhaps not as strong during the time, but certainly one to commend if my spirituality was anything to be compared with. We did freshman year together; he was wise, I was reckless but we still ended up with the same GPA (no hard feelings Alphonse).

Following my freshman year, I spent the summer holidays in Accra, Ghana . . . a decision that could have destroyed me altogether. One weeknight a friend was giving myself and another female friend a lift home. For some strange reason I decided to put on my seatbelt, something I rarely practiced. The friend in the driver's seat passed a remark as though to tease me saying "why you de fear? I shock for you". This, as I am sure you have already guessed, is slang for "why are you scared, you surprise me". Nonetheless, I wittingly brushed it off and kept my seatbelt fastened.

The ride was smooth as expected; he drove pretty well for a 5 foot 3 inches driver. However, only two minutes away from my house in the twenty minute long journey we collided at speeds in excess of 60mph with a vehicle travelling in the opposite direction. The airbags were out. The car was filled with smoke. The vehicle reeked of gasoline. At that very moment was when I had faced death for the first time in my life. I had excruciating pain in my back. Yet the pain was drowned by the screams and chants of bystanders panicking to rush the man in the other vehicle to the hospital—he was in desperate need of medical assistance.

The car was totaled. But I was not, and neither were my two friends involved in the collision. We escaped virtually unscathed and I had my mother pick us up from the scene of the accident. Mother was silent during the whole incident but deep within I perceived she was subtly praying to her God.

Later that night she called me to her room and gave me a shocking reminder of a prophesy her friend had made concerning my life three years prior to the incident. It was dreadfully accurate; from the description of the cars involved to the nature of the accident. As apprehensive as I was at the time, sophomore year quickly faded the reality of my near-death experience and I was back to my old ways.

The Encounter

October 2008; it was sophomore year. Alphonse had attended a church conference over the summer holidays and came back to the Bryant campus charged up to convert anyone and everyone. This boy had some nerve. One evening he categorically instructed me, respectfully, to stop listening to secular Hip Hop music. Now anyone who was remotely familiar with my years in high school would understand the absurdity of this instruction to me at the time. Hip Hop and Rap music was the central theme of my life; any song I heard more than twice would have the lyrics imprinted on my brain. That was my passion!

In high school, I was the entertainment prefect, the DJ for school parties, and was even part of a rap (comedy) group that made music for fun. Taking rap away from me would be imprisonment of my only form of creative expression. As you can imagine, this advice did not go down too well. Out of respect for Alphonse, I debated with him for countless hours making the case for why Hip Hop and Rap music should not be demonized in the manner in which it was. I lost, miserably. But that wasn't going to stop me from listening to Rap music.

One evening I entered Alphonse's room with the hope of simply hanging out and talking, which was commonplace during our university years. He was not there, I believe he was in a meeting but up until today, I still can't be sure. I found his iPod with earphones on his bed, and for some reason I cannot explain, found myself laying on his bed for three hours simply listening to Gospel music (that's all he had, nerd). Immediately I felt overwhelmed by the content and soul of the songs and it seemed I was taken to a different place for hours. Retrospectively, it sounds like a setup either of divine nature or otherwise, whereby there was no one in the room except the iPod and earphones carefully placed on the bed. Alphonse, was this your doing?

All the same, it got me saved. The following Sunday I agreed to attend church with Alphonse and made the public decision to forsake my own ways and make Jesus Christ my Lord. I have not looked back since. This resolution changed my life altogether. Collectively, Alphonse and I established a campus fellowship at Bryant University, with an extended arm conducted on Skype for others around the world. I have been invited to preach at several conferences in Accra and in the United Kingdom, and the blessings do not stop there. All glory goes to God for the work He has done in and through me.

The above testimony is not exhaustive of my life, experiences, and struggles and is certainly not meant to be. The motive was to grant you a glimpse of my past in order to appreciate any word written herein concerning God's goodness, purpose, and plan for His children.

Chapter 2

THE REAL MAN

Life in Christ was bliss . . . but challenging. I had to spend a great deal of social time explaining myself to old friends who simply could not come to terms with the new me. I don't blame them. Juxtaposing the old ragamuffin with the new souled out Christian was tough for anyone to swallow. Except for mother, of course. Undoubtedly, she was excited to witness the transformation of her son, but cunningly boasted of her expectancy, stating constantly that she knew without a shadow of a doubt a change would come to pass. And indeed it did, but not without a price.

This transformation cost me more than my precious time. I was losing friends, acquaintances, hobbies, and even my self-identity. The boy of old who was defined by rap music, the latest fashion, and anything that others would applaud as being 'cool' had suddenly lost interest in all of the above. Who was I now? I had been stripped of my identity. Worse still, I was taking eighteen credits during the fall semester of my sophomore year, which equates to a class in excess of the recommended five classes per semester. I had officially declared a double major at Bryant University with concentrations in Economics and Computer Information Systems. The pressure was on. The plethora of school work coupled with the countless hours dedicated to prayer, Bible study, fellowship, church, and the leisure reading of books by Christian authors was taking a toll on me. Something had got to give.

One night, out of desperation I got on my knees and casted doubt at the feet of God. The burden was immense and I found myself questioning whether it was all worth it. Why was I spending several hours of my day in service to God at the expense of my academic duties? There had to be more to life than just prayer and church, it seemed. At this time, in this moment of clarity, God revealed to me the true nature of man.

The Nature of Man

Man is spirit, soul, and body. Now, for the women's rights activist reading this book, I use the word 'man' as a unisex and universal term for mankind, which is generally consistent with biblical nomenclature. If you possess good attention to detail, you would notice that the sequence above is a tad atypical. The order was with intention. Mankind was created with a spirit, the eternal essence, a soul, the intellect and personality, and a body, the frame in which the spirit and soul coexist.

Of these three parts that constitute man, it would be beneficial to know that the spirit is of utmost importance. To understand the justification of this claim let us take it from the very beginning, Genesis.

> Then God said, "Let Us make man in Our image,
> according to Our likeness . . .
>
> **Genesis 1:26**

This verse taken out of the Bible indicates that all men are created in the image of God. Strangely, that would suggest by simple logic that all men ought to look the same. However, this does not appear to be the case. Evidently, humankind does have common characteristics amongst each other, hence the term 'man-kind'. Nevertheless there are some stark differences between all people. For one, there are no two people on earth who are completely identical, even identical twins. Secondly, geographical differences reveal vast differences between people in terms of race, hair texture, facial features, as well as a host of other differentiating factors. If indeed we were created in the bodily image of God, then which one of us would God resemble the most? Taking the verse above as a proposal of the idea that men were created in the physical image of God is not only a danger in creating racial dissension, but it is also outright unbiblical.

> God is spirit, and those who worship Him must worship in
> spirit and truth.
>
> **John 4:24**

This verse, taken out of the Gospel according to John, effectuates a change in perspective. I believe every verse in the Bible cannot be read in isolation—there is always another verse elsewhere that sheds more light on the subject matter. It is apparent from the scripture above that God is Spirit, which logically explains why He is invisible—go figure. Hence, if God is Spirit, then when He created mankind it would suggest that the spirit is the aspect of man that was created in the image of God.

Well, this revelation undeniably changes everything. Coming to the realization that you are first and foremost a spirit, with a soul, who lives in a body calls for a revision of priorities. Just as your body and soul require careful attention and grooming, likewise is the case with your spirit. I often come across men and women alike who direct a great deal of effort towards their body and soul, whilst entirely neglecting their spirit. Body building is good. A bottle-shaped body is flattering. A great mind is honorable. But a lean spirit is lethal.

It is a great shame that in today's world we have coined medical terms for conditions wherein people lack growth either physically in their body, or intellectually in their soul, but we disregard any lack in spirit. For instance, a teenager with the body of a toddler is often diagnosed with a growth disorder. Similarly, a mature person with an underdeveloped mental capacity is frequently diagnosed with mental retardation of some sort. However, when a mature person is spiritually destitute we refer to them as an intellectual—ironic isn't it? The spirit, if not more important than all other aspects of man, is at the very least as equally important, and deserves the same, if not more, level of attention and training as the soul and body. You can boast of a great body and mind, and amass all the wealth possible as a result of the two, but if your spirit is lean then all of the above is meaningless.

The Revelation

The discovery of the spirit-being as the real man granted me unfound comfort in knowing that the time and strength dedicated to serving God was not in vain. As I got off my knees, I reassured myself with this verse that recorded the very words of Jesus:

> But seek first His kingdom and His righteousness, and all
> these things will be added to you.
> **Matthew 6:33**

Indeed all other things were added to me. Although I dedicated much of my life to the things of God, the fall semester of my sophomore year was unbelievably successful. To date, my highest semester GPA of 3.83 occurred during that semester, in spite of the burden of an extra class, a double major, and numerous extra-curricular activities.

This is not a boast by any means, but a testament to the faithfulness of God. However, allow me to discount any notion that focusing purely on God whilst disregarding your academic, employment, or secular obligations will result in any success. It will not. Complacency is typical in places such as Ghana, my native country, where believers remain reactive, rather than proactive, and simply comfort themselves with axioms that are often taken out of context—"Nyame bë yë", which means "God will do it" in the Twi dialect. God will not do anything until you give Him a reason to. Remember, a faith with works is the only faith that works.

> For just as the body without the spirit is dead, so also faith
> without works is dead.
>
> **James 2:26**

Chapter 3

IN PLANE SIGHT

I am well aware that the spelling of the chapter heading above is unusual; in case you were thinking otherwise, may I take this opportunity to inform you that it is not a typographical error, Einstein. As the content of the chapter is unveiled, you will come to an understanding of the true meaning of this title.

Sophomore year was definitely a year of victory, success, and spiritual growth. It was also a year of loneliness, seclusion, and boredom. Now make no mistake—I was not bored or lonely due to the lack of companionship. I had many friends and people I would fellowship with on a daily basis. The feeling of isolation was not due to the lack of social interaction, but rather as a result of the contrast in worldview that existed between myself and others. For instance, any given day on the Bryant University campus called for excessive drinking, sexual activities, clubbing, and riotous teens screaming "let's get wasted!" Clearly, there was a gulf between my outlook on life and that of the majority of students enrolled at the university. I had developed a self-awareness of sin, whereas for most people I came across, turpitude was a nonentity.

To top it off, most days and nights I would get the impression that there was a dark presence in my dorm room. It was not ubiquitous enough to be frightening but it was unquestionably significant enough to be noticeable. Some nights I would wake up from sleep in panic and spend some time in prayer just to reassure myself that the dark presence was harmless. This episode of my life in Christ most certainly tested my faith—if I had made the decision to step into the Light, why did God allow me to be intimidated by darkness? Was the feeling of loneliness necessary, or was this all part of some grand plan of God? The experience opened my eyes to the reality of how faith operates.

You Are Not Alone

God never promised a trial-free life, nor did He promise a journey without obstacles. A thorough read of the scriptures discloses that God only vowed that He would be present through the storm. Time and again, we develop the perception that God is absent when we go through tribulations, but a gentle reminder of the faithfulness of God can be found in the words of the Psalmist.

> Even though I walk through the valley of the shadow of death,
> I fear no evil, for You are with me . . .
> **Psalm 23:4**

This verse is surely not foreign to anyone who has been remotely exposed to the precepts of Judeo-Christian beliefs. The excerpt of poetry encapsulates the very idea that even in the darkest moment, at the gloomiest hour, in the toughest situation, the presence of God remains your fortress. Now these words of encouragement might sound nice and dandy but in all sincerity, it's pretty difficult to see God when you are nose deep in the flood. However, this is the phase in which your faith is tested.

I believe there is a vivid parallel between our experience during troubled times, and sitting on a plane for a cross-border flight. You see, when you make the decision to board a trans-Atlantic flight, for instance, you are placing your confidence in the pilot to get you from point A to point B, and to get you there safely. The amusing part of this decision-making process is that you probably disregard any assessment of the credibility of the pilot. Not once do you request a copy of the captain's aviation license to verify that he or she is indeed authorized to fly the plane. In actual fact, for most flights you likely never get a glimpse of the pilot but still comfort yourself with the silent faith that there is actually one in the cockpit—how can you be sure there is a pilot on the plane if you never get to see him? Furthermore, in the period of air turbulence, it would surprise you that the confidence that you place in the pilot, if indeed there is one, keeps you calm as the plane rides through the storm.

I find that the faith we place in the unseen pilot during air turbulence would be very useful if placed in the unseen God during the turmoil of life. While the plane is travelling through an area of air turbulence, I am convinced that it would definitely alarm you if you saw the pilot walk leisurely down the aisles of the cabin checking up on the well-being of passengers. "Who's in the driver's seat?" you would fearfully think. Likewise, in the season of trials and teething troubles, rest assured that the feeling of God's absence is misleading; He is simply taking care of issues from the cockpit.

The Peaceful Storm

Upon speaking to several Christians who were at one point new converts to the faith, I came to the realization that the dark presence and intimidation was commonplace. Despite the ups and downs that characterized my second year in university, the testing of my faith had negated any misconceptions regarding the presence of God or the lack thereof during trying times. The storm did not break me, it only produced endurance.

> . . . knowing that the testing of your faith produces endurance
> **James 1:3**

Chapter 4

PURPOSE DRIVEN

I made the choice to spend the fall semester of my junior year studying abroad at the University College of London (UCL) in the United Kingdom. The aim was to bolster my CV with international and cross-culture experience, and where better to do so than in a city considered the melting pot of the world. Alright I lied, you caught me. The decision to study abroad was simply fueled by my desire to be closer to the love of my life at the time. Yes, I'm a sucker for love. Don't judge.

London was great. It afforded me the opportunity to catch up with family and old mates from high school. Of course, there was always that awkward moment when an old friend would start a conversation about hot girls and realize midway that I was a changed man. "So . . . I hear you're now a man of God" they would ask, in a miserable attempt to change the topic of discussion. To curtail the tension, I would usually smirk and pretend I did not notice their embarrassment. Surprisingly, I actually enjoyed those ungraceful moments—it amused me when I witnessed the awkwardness of friends when it came to my new found faith.

While some buddies passed gawky comments in the name of friendly banter, other mates made remarks in conversation that were purely distasteful. One weekend as I was paying my lady a visit at the University of Warwick where she studied Law, I bumped into an old classmate from high school. From my days as a young vagabond until then, I had always held this gentleman in high esteem due to his diligence in academics and enterprising leadership. At the entrance of Costcutter, there stood two old time friends in hysterics catching up on the lost years. And then just so casually he uttered these words, "I hear you're a pastor now, what the hell is wrong with you man?" He was still laughing, but I wasn't. The hysteria immediately wore off and was converted into a feeling of discomfort. I was certainly not amused but for the sake of a peaceable friendship I retained a smile on my face, albeit one with clenched teeth. This experience taught me an invaluable lesson that propelled me into the path of my calling.

The Motivation

In every aspect of life, you would invariably end up making a fool of yourself if you are driven by the applause of men rather than your specific purpose. The truth is that human beings are psychologically inconsistent creatures whereby an act applauded today would surprisingly be condemned tomorrow. If you were to base your actions solely on man's response, it is likely your values, ideologies, and morals would change on a daily basis. The fact of the matter is that all men, especially those who consider themselves children of God, must be motivated by purpose alone.

The word purpose is defined as the reason for which something exists, is done, made or used. Therefore purpose can be understood as the very essence of a thing. I believe all men were created with purpose for the below is what God proclaims through the prophet Jeremiah:

> "For I know the plans that I have for you"
> declares the LORD . . .
> **Jeremiah 29:11**

I am not sure if I speak for everyone, but it is comforting and encouraging to know that God has a plan, and one that is categorically designed for me. It provides purpose, hope, and direction. The only issue however, is that the specific plan, which is of good and not of evil, is not inscribed in black and white. To clarify, there is no verse in the Bible like William 2:5 that says "you must become a carpenter, declares the LORD". Or Kofi 1:1 that reads "accept the position at that law firm in New York". The scriptures provide no specificity in regards to individuals concerning their purpose and the plan of God for their life.

Does this cause a problem? Perhaps—but only for those who do not seek God.

> The LORD has looked down from heaven upon the sons
> of men to see if there are any who understand,
> [any] who seek after God
>
> **Psalm 14:2**

This verse suggests that understanding and seeking God earnestly are in tandem. You see, if you want to come to an understanding of how something truly works, it would benefit you to get in contact with the manufacturer. Suppose you purchased a BMW M5 and a few days after use, it encountered a fault. The wise thing to do would be to contact the manufacturer to report the problem and get an appreciation of how the vehicle operates. After a checkup, you discover that you have been using this car as a goods carrier for heavy products in your business, rather than its intended purpose as a pseudo sports car.

The same analogy can be applied to our relationship with God. In order to appreciate the purpose with which you were specifically created, it is imperative to seek the Creator. The unfortunate problem with many Christians today is that we often take our strengths and interests as the gold standard for determining God's purpose for our lives—this is not only deceptive but can also be severely dangerous.

Let me give you a few examples of what I mean. Let's start with the Son of God Himself, Jesus Christ. Now in case you were unaware, Jesus was a man with a very simple CV—born in Bethlehem, studied carpentry, and worked as a carpenter. That's about it. He was neither employed at Goldman Sachs nor did He have an amazing education among the elite. We can assume He was, at the least, decent at carpentry otherwise He probably would not have been known as a carpenter in all Judea. However, due to His close relationship with The Father, He understood the gravity of the purpose He had been assigned; to forsake His career as a superstar carpenter and carry the sins of the world to death on a cross. By virtue of the cognizance of His purpose, we are graced with salvation as a result.

Similarly, my mother is an incredible cook. She makes the best corned beef Jollof rice—except when she puts carrots in it. I hate carrots. In any case, I would consider it ludicrous if she pursued a career as a chef purely as a consequence of her magnificent culinary skills. Simply because her strength lies in that arena does not imply that God has called her to be a chef. I for one am a superb soccer player—shout out to all the haters. Alright perhaps not superb, but it is undoubtedly an area of competence for me. However, I am certain with all manner of conviction that I have not been called into professional sports. Why? Because I have plugged into the heart of my Creator who has revealed His purpose for my life.

Purpose Breeds Contempt

The moment others become aware of your purpose, it would benefit you emotionally to expect some hate mail. Recall when Jesus informed the Jews that He was purposed to be the Savior of the world? Immediately they began following Him from city to city with the sole intention to accuse Him of blasphemy and tarnish His reputation amongst the Jews. But the fierce opposition did not stop Him, it couldn't.

The uncouth remark made by my old friend taught me this lesson about purpose: the plan of God for my life is divorced from both the applause of men and their discouraging words. At the end of the day, the ultimate Judge is God and it is He that we strive to please. To recount the words of the new NBA prodigy, Jeremy Lin: "I remind myself I'm playing for God; it relieves me of all pressure".

> For am I now seeking the favor of men, or of God? Or am I
> striving to please men? If I were still trying to please men,
> I would not be a bond-servant of Christ.
> **Galatians 1:10**

Chapter 5

SACRIFICE

The move to the British tertiary education system forced a change in attitude towards my academic work. Even though I was studious during my time in the States, I believe the nature of the American curriculum allowed for nothing else. At Bryant University, there was continuous assessment every week testing your mastery of the subject matter. Therefore, if indeed you wanted to excel, the never-ending tests, projects, and exams kept you abreast with the material.

England was different, and shockingly so. It was all about independent study and self-assessment. For every class I enrolled in there was one exam, and possibly two assessments that had no impact whatsoever on my final grade but were still compulsory. Could someone kindly explain the logic behind that—I still don't get it. In any case, that one exam served as a terrifying reminder that there was only one chance; it was do or die.

Although the experience abroad was purposed to be one of fun, leisure, and relaxation, there ended up being a lot more pressure on me than previously thought. Not only did I have to ensure that I adjusted properly to the new methodology of assessment, but I was also required to certify that I kept up to speed with the assigned reading, familiarized myself with past papers, and completed any other academic obligations in a self-regulatory manner. Professors no longer doled out responsibilities—I had to figure out what was required independently, and then complete it. All this had to be done in conjunction with ministerial duties, in which I directed a weekly fellowship at my hall of residence and assisted the UCL campus ministry with their daily activities. And of course, I had to make time for the lady—how could I forget.

This degree of sacrifice was alien to me. I spent all of my time serving others and none on myself. I had been wearing the same sneakers for a year and a half, something I would historically upgrade routinely. The bulk of my finances either went into serving God or helping others out. Or Chinese food. I love Chinese food.

One weekend in November, I found myself in Milton Keynes paying my sister a visit at my aunt's house where she was lodging during a ten day trip to the United Kingdom. We had great laughs and reminisced about childhood moments. Sunday came, and I informed them that I would have to make my way to the train station shortly in order to arrive in London early enough for the fellowship which I led. Unexpectedly, both my aunt and sister started whining, putting forth the argument that it would be our last time in each other's company for a long while. They simply did not want me to leave. Admittedly, I had no desire to head back to London either—in Milton Keynes I enjoyed the love of family, free home-cooked food, cable television, and the comfort of a home. At that moment, the unflattering box I called a dorm room was not looking very appealing. Nonetheless, I remembered the mandate I agreed to, to put others first continually, knowing that my sacrifice for God and others was not in vain. I packed up and set off for London.

Sacrifice Releases Power

A universal principle I have adopted into my philosophical beliefs is that sacrifice releases power and is always rewarded. Sacrifice is meaningless unless it is complemented with the correct attitude towards it. Sacrifice is defined as the surrender or destruction of something prized or desirable for the sake of something considered as having a higher or more pressing claim. In layman's terms, this means giving up something that costs you for something else held in higher regard. As expected, this definition is consistent with scripture.

" . . . for I will not offer burnt offerings to the
LORD my God which cost me nothing."
2 Samuel 24:24

Christians today are sadly obsessed with calling self-deprivation a sacrifice when it does not cost them a thing. During the period of Lent, I often hear Christians pass comments with pride such as "I gave up chocolate for Lent" or "I am not going to watch Family Guy during this period". I am inclined to think these statements would sound absurd to a God who gave His only begotten Son as a sacrifice for all. How about giving up that sin you dearly love? Perhaps that would be a more worthy sacrifice.

Friends, anything that does not cost you is not a sacrifice. Many believers do not witness the power of God being manifested in their lives due to this simple reality: the lack of sacrifice.

I believe it is fair to say that the greatest example of sacrifice can be found in the personhood of Jesus Christ, and the power released as a result is evident even until today. The ransom He paid on the cross was not only relevant to cover the sins of those who lived during His time, but still carries the power to transform bona fide sinners like myself today. Imagine, two thousand years after His execution He remains the most talked about Person in the world, the individual with the largest number of books written about them, and also boasts an impressive following of an estimated two billion people. And the award for the most popular Person goes to? You guessed it.

The thing to note however is that if Jesus had not made the decision to fulfill His mandate and commit to the sacrifice on the cross, His story and fame would have been hugely different today. The Gospel is one of love and sacrifice, and the product is the discharge of power.

> For the word of the cross is foolishness to those who are
> perishing, but to us who are being saved it is the power of God.
> **1 Corinthians 1:18**

Sacrifice is key in our service to the King. Christ commanded all men who wish to proclaim His Lordship to embrace sacrifice as an instrument of worship and dedication:

> Then Jesus said to His disciples, "If anyone wishes to
> come after Me, he must deny himself,
> and take up his cross and follow Me.
> **Mathew 16:24**

I believe pop culture has misunderstood this verse. When Jesus said take up your cross, I do not believe I am mistaken in thinking that He was not referring to a physical gold cross with diamonds on it, or 'bling' as it is called amongst the youth today. If it was so, then God would never be pleased with me, but would rather be delighted with the rappers who boast the largest crosses on their necklaces. After all, they are taking up fairly weighty crosses in comparison to you and I.

As amusing as the analogy above sounds, the cross that Christ was referring to here was not a physical one but rather a burden of self-denial. The context of this instruction leads us to believe that as followers, we must die to our selfish ambitions and conceited ways, and drink from the cup of sacrifice to serve God and others. I have made it a personal goal never to wear a cross on my neck if I do not bear one on my back.

Interestingly, the consequence of sacrifice is not specific to the context of spirituality. As I mentioned before, sacrifice is a universal phenomenon. I once heard a wise young man say that a vision without sacrifice is simply a daydream, which I found to be true.

Take a random list of revered people in the world and determine the factors that they all have in common. Surely, one of the factors common to them all is their risk appetite—they were risk takers and sacrificial in nature. Let's briefly examine the life of Bill Gates for example, a man who gave up the security of an education at the prestigious Harvard University to pursue a career in computer software. Today, he is arguably the most successful person in terms of material wealth amassed. Another example would be Martin Luther King, a civil rights activist whose sacrifice cost him his dear life in the fight for racial equality. In his honor, the third Monday of January each year is declared Martin Luther King Jr. Day in celebration of his life. This is the power of sacrifice.

The Fruit of Sacrifice

Meanwhile, back in London I was running up and down doing the work of God whilst simultaneously trying to excel as a student. Countless sacrifices were made in favor of my ministerial duties as fellow classmates were leaving a trail of dust in the race for internship programs and graduate jobs. They were all far ahead in the application process and left me to scramble with the vultures for the few places left.

This situation was not a problem for the God I served at all. In the month of February, I was informed that I had secured an internship as an analyst with a Wall Street investment bank in London. As if this news was not rewarding enough, my certificate from UCL with the results of my semester abroad arrived with an overall 2:1 grade and a first in one of my Economics modules. There, laid in plain sight, was the fruit of my sacrifice.

> Therefore, my beloved brethren, be steadfast, immovable,
> always abounding in the work of the Lord, knowing that
> your toil is not in vain in the Lord.
>
> **1 Corinthians 15:58**

Chapter 6

OH WORD?

My arrival to the Bryant University campus following my semester abroad in London brought about new contests. Sure, unlike other peers I had no anxieties about internships and graduate jobs as I had already secured a position. However, I was immensely burdened to witness friends I initially fellowshipped with adopting the social culture of the student body. Raving, foul music, alcoholism, and sexual play was the order of the day. Where did I go wrong? Was I not praying with enough fervency for others?

Perhaps I was too hard on myself. I often took it upon myself as a personal failure whenever I encountered the backslidden. What troubled me the most was the profane clatter they called music—I know, the cheek of it coming from me, right? I admit, in my dorm room on Friday nights I would habitually overhear the music from parties being held in neighboring dorm suites. Occasionally, a throwback song will start playing and in response, everyone would chant uncontrollably. I often found myself subconsciously singing along to the songs that were familiar to my childhood days. Midway through the song, my eyes would gape open and lips ajar in horrific realization of the meaning behind the lyrics.

For instance, one weeknight the song Sweat by Inner Circle caught my ears from the dorm room of an insufferable resident and I began recounting the lyrics of the song in reminiscence of musical chairs, a game regularly played during my childhood years. Come on, don't pretend to be holier than thou, you know the song! Fine, you asked for it: "Girl I wanna' make you sweat, sweat till you can't sweat no more, and if you cry out, I'm going to push it some more". Shockingly, as a seven year old in Accra singing along to the words I had no bearing of the message behind it. I honestly thought it was pertinent to beach sports, possibly in relation to the music video.

As a product of the nineties, TLC was my favorite R&B group and to date I can recite their greatest hits verbatim. At the tender age of eight, I knew the lyrics to their breakthrough hit Creep, only to discover fourteen years later as I pondered on the words that the theme was a promotion of infidelity. Goodness, the vast number of perverse words that have escaped my mouth as a child through the medium of music is mind boggling.

At this time, it appeared I was wearing the hat of Alphonse who historically demonized secular Hip Hop, and rightly so. The experience I had in conversation with believers concerning music of this nature was undeniably eye-opening, as they diligently searched for any justification possible regarding the content and soul of the songs. Truthfully, many of the arguments made would sound justifiable to the untrained ear, but to me they were merely flimsy excuses. The most disturbing appeal I heard from advocates of uncouth secular music was this: "it's just words, I only like the beat". This reasoning posits the distressing idea that words are meaningless. Are they really? Let's examine this from a biblical perspective.

The Power of Words

Our words are the most valuable commodity we have as human beings as they define our worldview, character, and even our future. It is critical that men and women, especially those with a Kingdom perspective, come to an understanding of the significance of the spoken and written word. Looking through the lens of Genesis we can appreciate the fact that God created all things solely through His spoken word.

Then God said, "Let there be light"; and there was light.

Genesis 1:3

This excerpt of scripture is one that is profusely cited by many but seldom understood. In the emptiness and void of eternity past, God spoke a few words and created the world as we know it. Throughout the first chapter of Genesis, we observe the creative power of God illustrated through the words He spoke. Now, if the Bible leads us correctly in believing that we were created in the image of God, it proposes the very idea that our words possess the power to create and to destroy. Perhaps an example is in order to shed more light on this assertion.

In April of the year 2012, my native country was shaken with an uprising that threatened to invade the peace and security of Ghana. The nation was taken aback in light of the optimism that the international community had placed in my homeland as a beacon of hope in a region of West Africa that had been long plagued with power struggles and violence. I was certainly surprised to learn that the unrest was caused by three simple words: "I declare war".

A frustrated member of the opposition party deemed it fit to share his antipathy on national radio, singling out an ethnic group he threatened to inflict harm upon. Within hours, the capital city was in outrage. The amusing thing is that this antagonist had neither the clout nor the authority to declare war, thereby apparently making his statement futile. However, we discover here that his words were in actual fact meaningful and held the power to destroy the tranquility enjoyed for several years.

It is imperative, therefore, that we have a revelation of the sheer power with which we have been endowed. The words we speak and those we listen to define the fruit of our labor—either we are being constructive or destructive.

> Death and life are in the power of the tongue . . .
> **Proverbs 18:21**

The adage from the book of Proverbs epitomizes this discussion. Imagine, Jesus died and resurrected such that we might receive everlasting life, but this verse implies the notion that life can be found in the power of the tongue. I find it truly refreshing that the works of Christ fulfill ancient scripture. The reason is the following. Indeed, Christ Jesus in His capacity as the Son of God died on the cross and arose from the dead that our sins may be atoned for and further that we may receive eternal life. However, please understand that His death and resurrection was only an offer that required acceptance on our part in order for the contract of salvation to be established. Contract law stipulates that a contract is void unless an offer and an acceptance has been made. This protocol holds true in salvation.

Salvation is an offer which awaits the acceptance of mankind as a prerequisite for eternal life to be realized. For this reason the Apostle Paul writes in his letter to the Romans:

> If you confess with your mouth Jesus as Lord, and believe in
> your heart that God raised Him from the dead,
> you will be saved.
> **Romans 10:9**

Hence, life indeed lies in the power of the tongue as the book of Proverbs specifies because there is a condition of confession which involves words. In light of this truth, we can safely make the declaration that we have been saved by our words. This modifies our entire perspective doesn't it? If we can receive the gift of life by means of a sincere heart and our words of confession, then logically the same should hold true for the contrary: we can also be ruined by words.

Kill the Beat

The words of man should be maintained to the highest standard possible as, all things considered, they signify the substance of our integrity. Consider the men and women who are appointed into civil service and public office. Their demonstration of commitment to the interests of their nation is portrayed through the words they are required to utter during their swearing in ceremony. Likewise, even simpletons who testify in court are urged to publicly announce their vow to speak the truth during legal proceedings. When all's said and done, our words represent the only currency acceptable as a down payment on our veracity. Jesus appears to subscribe to this mentality as recorded in the Gospels.

> Heaven and earth will pass away, but My words will not pass away.
> **Matthew 24:35**

For the majority of Christians today, subscription to this principle seems not to extend to the context of music. We cannot afford to be casual with our attitude towards music and musical content as it is an instrument of great influence on the masses. If God created all things for His glory, it wouldn't be considered naïve to believe that He expects music endorsed by His children to glorify Him. Yet, this is far from the case. In fact from my personal experience, not only does some of the music Christians approve of not glorify God, but it acts in direct hostility to His statutes and precepts.

Permit me to tackle this argument from the vantage point of the youth. It pierces my heart to state that God is not the chief influence on our youth. Neither is it our parents nor teachers. It isn't money, friends or television. In reality you would be mistaken to even think it was the opposite sex. The greatest influence on our youth is music.

As a teenager in high school, Hip Hop and Rap music was the soundtrack to my life. I was so heavily engrossed in this genre of music that my passion led me to the office of entertainment prefect in sixth form. I was also the DJ at school parties and was involved in music making with a group of close associates as previously cited in my testimony. In retrospect, the content and soul of secular Rap steered me to an appreciation of all sorts of evils, some of which are too perverse to disclose—my mother could potentially be reading this. Nonetheless to provide a vague idea, the genre impacted my treatment of females as objects of pleasure, my attitude to violence, lust for wealth, and certainly instilled pride in my heart.

Pride was the most obvious fruit of Hip Hop. The high school I attended boasted advanced facilities and was somewhat blessed to be liberal and upbeat. During break time, seniors would often play Rap music in the canteen as all the students relaxed and enjoyed their lunch. It was fascinating to especially see male students change their gait, posture, and entire character as they strolled into the canteen, reciting the lyrics of the song playing. Within a matter of a split second, the swagger they had forgotten to put on in the morning suddenly appeared in response the music, shrugging their shoulders as though they'd just been crowned king. This mannerism, one that I am confident most youthful readers would identify with, is a product of the pride infused by music of this nature. The startling thing is that not only is the egotism produced by Hip Hop destructive in community building, but it is also obstructive in our relationship with God.

Ghetto Fabulous

The words in our music command the power to destroy. This claim is not only scripturally sound, but is also evidentially convincing. It burdens my heart to witness the moral corruption and financial impoverishment in the ghettos and projects of America that clothe themselves with the culture of Hip Hop. The rappers preach about matters concerning money, women, cars, clothes, gang violence, and other material possessions, imbuing the multitudes in these places with a desire to acquire this chaff. These same rappers then sheepishly relocate to suburbia with the riches acquired from the proceeds of their music whilst leaving those they encouraged in sin to continue killing themselves over a difference in area codes.

For those who condone their content, they are simply left with false promises of satisfaction from amassing wealth and sleeping with as many of the opposite sex as possible. In fact, Hip Hop causes them to dig deeper into their poverty. Their strong desire for material possessions spurred by the influence of this music often leads shallow listeners to compulsive spending even in cases where they lack the financial clout to afford such items. It is sad to see the poor borrowing money to purchase a pair of Air Jordan sneakers in an attempt to impress others, when in such situations investments should be made to secure a more promising future.

Music is not just an instrument of entertainment. It is a lifestyle. Consider any culture in the world. Each culture has its own distinct language and music that they pride themselves in; this holds true for even the most indigenous cultures. That said, it would make sense to claim that the language you speak and music you make—amongst other factors of course—define your culture. This is the reason why the language spoken through secular Rap and Hip Hop music has created a culture of disrespect of authority, provocative speech, promiscuity, and other ails that have led to moral degradation in the society of our youth. The result is an elimination of peace, disruption of prosperity, breakdown of relationships, and a complete destruction of communities.

The pride infused by means of this genre serves as an obstruction to a healthy relationship with God as well.

> Therefore it says, "God is opposed to the proud,
> but gives grace to the humble"
> **James 4:6**

A proud heart repels God. Imagine, if the One who created the universe is fighting against you on the other team, who would be left standing? Humility is the fundamental posture any Christian ought to take in their dealings with God and with men. The unfortunate truth is the culture of Hip Hop does not allow for that. It is noticeable even in the church setting: those who are influenced by a great deal of Rap music hardly flinch during the praise and worship part of the service—they are diplomatic in all their affairs. I must admit, I fall into this category but I am poised to change.

Now, I beseech you not to misinterpret this chapter as an attempt to demonize Hip Hop music and Rap. Truthfully, I am opposed to the generalization of this genre. I speak specifically of Hip Hop by virtue of my close association with the culture and the knowledge I possess of the musical content. However, any genre that advocates a message that is anti-scripture will merit the same reaction.

The reason I am opposed to the generalization of Hip Hop and Rap is because a distinction can be made in the content and soul of different songs. The advent of Christian rappers is making progress in changing the orthodox Christian perception that music of the nature cannot be used to glorify God. Indeed it can. As I came to the realization that I was blessed with the musical gift, I changed the content of my lyrics to that which was Christ centered. Allow me to share with you the path to my salvation in lyrical format.

Beautiful Truth

When I look at my life from the genesis
I can say that I really know what blessing is
The world and its lust I used to mess with it
Couldn't get enough of them as far as all the pleasures went
Heard a lot of talk, but mostly mixed messages
Said I should come to Christ, but man was I hesitant
They say the Love of God has no measurement
Rejecting it, to the Lord Jesus I never went
I was lord of my life, I was president
People talked but this boy wasn't listening
My sin trapped me—they call it imprisonment
I was a slave to my pride, it was sickening
Yet the Risen King, whilst I lived in sin
Came to save me so now I could live in Him
He was Heaven sent, and put to death for men
That's why I write, because He said we should be fishing men

He's knocking at your door will you let Him in?
I'm not the best but He made me a better man
I'm not trying to get rich or be on Letterman
Forget wealth, it's His Word I put my treasures in

I'm not the best of men, but I am clever than
Most men because I read His New Testament
The Old Testament, so many lessons learnt
His arms open wide, He is gesturing
He's saying "come to me, my child run to Me"
"My life on the cross—look what they've done to Me"
"I died a death you couldn't die, it wasn't fun to Me"
"But rose again so that you could be a son to Me"
"I am Truth, I am Hope, I am Life"
"I will shine in the dark, I am Light"
"I'm trying to save you, why are you trying to muscle Me"
"The great I AM, I need you to put your trust in Me"

Word Up

That was sexy wasn't it?

Permit me to leave you with this final thought: if you are a Christian who happens to be a rapper, then be a Christian rapper—do not put the rapper first, and include the Christian as an add-on. This applies to all other professions as well. Bear in mind that we are first and foremost Christ followers and any other activity in word or deed must follow suit.

And no, I am not suggesting that as Christians all our products and materials should bear the name of Christ on them; that would be absurd and, if I may speak freely, utterly boring. Needless to say, the fruit of our labor should not be in hostility to God, but should rather seek to glorify Him.

Chapter 7

THE RATIONALITY OF FAITH

The season was Fall, the month was August, and the year was 2010—I was back on the Bryant campus following my summer internship in London for the fourth and final year of my tenure as an undergrad. I had been promised many things in my life, but never was I assured that I would approach senior year with a respectable grade point average and a full time offer upon graduation. Better still, I was bestowed with the coveted honor of being resident assistant, a leadership position supplemented with free room and board thereby reducing my living expenses by $12,000 per year. Now, anyone from my neck of the woods would identify with my excitement—that was not pocket change.

The role of resident assistant can be fairly challenging for a deep-seated Christian. The nature of events and activities in promotion of the campus' core values were often congruent with my beliefs, but at other times were in direct conflict. For instance, the Christian dogma concerning sexuality clearly influences my predisposition against homosexuality. However, I also strongly speak against homophobia for the sole reason that it is not an act of godly love. Hence, my conscience allowed me to support campus-wide campaigns against the unfair treatment of those who identified themselves as gay and lesbians. Nonetheless, I found myself in a sticky situation during times we were encouraged to distribute free condoms to the resident population in promotion of safe sex.

Like, really? During a Friday fellowship meeting I would preach on the consequences of fornication from a biblical perspective, then on Saturday night this same preacher would be expected to share condoms to those he ministered to . . . incredible.

As a resident assistant, I belonged to the Upper Village staff—they were a great group of guys I tell you. But Of course, I happened to be the only radical Christian in my assigned staff, in the midst of many agnostics and a couple of atheists. Interestingly, the staff member whose company I enjoyed the most was a bona fide atheist. For the purposes of this discussion let's call him Max. This young man was the embodiment of a true resident assistant—he was helpful, kind, and allowed himself to be inconvenienced for the sake of others. Undeniably, he was unassuming and gracious. But he had a prevalent disinterest and repugnance for the things of God.

One Friday night both Max and I were on duty doing rounds on campus. Unlike most duty nights, Max spent his time between rounds in my dorm room and like the opportunist I am, we engaged in conversation regarding religious matters for over three hours. It was an enlightening experience. All things considered, if I lacked grounding in doctrine and theology, Max would have effortlessly convinced me that the concept of God was manufactured by man—his arguments were compelling.

Max was raised Catholic and spent many of his younger years in church. He attended a Catholic high school as well, but although he was churched, he lacked an authentic relationship with God. During his late teens he developed a rebellious heart for the house of God and even became doubtful of the existence of God. A few years later, based on circumstantial events that took place in his life and the Catholic church, the captivating argument for atheism convinced him to adopt the school of thought that a God simply does not exist.

During RA training, the period in which upcoming resident assistants were equipped with the skills and tools to excel as role models on campus, the entire staff was educated on the true meaning of success, as presented by a priest. Upon conclusion of the presentation, the resident director asked for the staff's thoughts on the content in an attempt to solicit our views and opinions. A fellow female resident assistant decided to bless the entire staff with these marvelous words: "although it was religious and everything, I really enjoyed it". I wondered, was that really necessary? It appeared that the antagonism against anything remotely religious had become a contagion across the campus.

Max and I were enrolled in the same Public Speaking class during the second semester of senior year. I reckoned that this class afforded

me the stage to publicly defend people of faith as encouraged by the
Apostle Peter:

> But sanctify Christ as Lord in your hearts, always being ready
> to make a defense to everyone who asks you to
> give an account for the hope that is in you,
> yet with gentleness and reverence.
>
> **1 Peter 3:15**

And that's exactly what I did. For my final speech, I argued the case
for why faith should be encouraged and not shunned. This chapter is a
reproduction of that speech, but I will preamble the discussion with a
disclaimer: this is not an attempt to prove the existence of God; there is
an exhaustive amount of literature in that regard. The sole aim of this
section is to provide a defense for faith from a rational perspective, and
to encourage those who once believed to reconsider where they choose
to place their trust.

Faith is Universal

Let's begin by defining the concept of faith with the help of our
friends from Oxford. The dictionary definition of faith is as follows:
belief, trust, confidence. In essence faith means to believe, trust, or have
confidence in something or someone. Faith tends to be associated with
religion, but I dare to make the assertion that faith is experienced more
outside the context of religion than within. Permit me to demonstrate
my reasoning. Have you ever seen your heart? I presume not, but yet you
believe with absolute certainty that indeed there is a heart beating inside
your chest. Likewise we have never laid eyes on our brains have we?
Nonetheless, to date I have met no man who is the least bit uncertain as
to the presence of a brain inside his cranium. It is solely by faith that we
agree to the anatomical description of man that science presents.

In the same vein, when was the last time you boarded a plane and
requested to verify the aviation license of the pilot? Or perhaps the driver's
license of the taxi driver you hired? The food license of the restaurant you
dined at? There exists in every man and woman a silent and unconscious
faith that keeps us at ease in our everyday dealings and operations.
Interestingly, we tend to underestimate our own level of faith.

Faith is universal, unprejudiced. Faith does not discriminate between
the Christian, Muslim or even the atheist. But of course, there are those
who disagree with the faith doctrine, but let's examine what these
opponents of faith have to say.

Richard Dawkins, a prolific leader and author of atheist doctrine writes in his book, *The God Delusion*: "When few people are delusional, it is called insanity. When many people are delusional, it is called religion". The writer continues to make the case that faith is belief without any evidence and should be eradicated by all means. However, in light of the universality of faith, this argument is a tad worrisome as faith is extra-religious.

A minister and scholar in the eighteenth century, Charles Finney, put it this way: "The little child, for instance, lives by faith. Human society exists by faith; destroy all confidence, all faith, and society could not exist; and no business would be transacted" Now, to provide some perspective, why would you sign a contract with a counterparty if you had no faith they would adhere to the terms of the contract and deal in good faith? Similarly, what encourages a husband to remain faithful to his spouse if he has no faith in her attitude to commitment? Truly, faith is not as meaningless as the secular society has attempted to paint it.

In the account of Richard Dawkins he also denounced faith as irrational and praised academia as a more rational alternative to faith. Yet, in my personal experience with academia I have discovered the untruth in this statement—academia is just as fallible when it comes to rationality. For instance, in a Business Ethics class we deprecate Nike for maltreating its workers in Taiwan like animals. In this same college, we are taught in a Biology class that human beings actually are animals. Thus, on what basis do we condemn Nike's malpractices? In my opinion, this too is irrational. But we believe the twaddle thrown us by professors, and why? Possibly due to the fact that we place our faith in academia to be accurate, rational, and faultless.

Finally, in an attempt to veto religiosity, skeptics contend that faith is dangerous, citing numerous atrocities done in the name of faith such as the crusades in the eleventh century and the Twin Tower attacks in New York. In no way do I discount the fact that these actions ought to be condemned. However, I believe that the rejection of something due to the potential harm it may inflict is brutally poor judgment. Folks, if faith led to the events of 9-11 and is thus deemed dangerous, well I wouldn't be foolish to believe that physics and chemistry led to the atomic bomb that wiped out populations—does this suggest that the discipline of science in particular should be discontinued? Certainly not. I believe that most will agree that physics is essential. Likewise with faith. You see, fire has the power to destroy buildings and tear apart families. Nonetheless, fire also provides us with warmth and a source of heat for cooking, amongst various other amenities. Faith in and of itself is not dangerous; it is the manner in which it is used that poses potential harm.

The key proponents of faith over the centuries bear testament to the sheer importance of faith in the construction of the social fabric we call the 21st century. Imagine, were it not for the faith that Martin Luther King had in God, I as a person of color, and indeed others like me, would not be graced with the opportunity to attend educational institutions of global repute. Likewise, without the faith of the Catholic Church, many hospitals, schools, and institutions would have never been established to advance the wellbeing of society. In fact, were it not for the faith you placed in this book, I doubt you would have sacrificially churned out ten dollars to make the purchase (shame on you if you jumped on the freebie bandwagon).

The truth is we all possess more faith than we perceive. Contrary to popular belief, faith is not a mystical aura that religious people use to comfort themselves in trying times. Faith exists outside the context of religion. Every living being has faith; the only difference is where we decide to direct this faith. For instance, the Christian places his faith in Jesus Christ, the Muslim in Allah, and the atheist in his or herself. Indeed, faith is the common ground between all men irrespective of race, creed, nationality, or language.

Dear friends, I have not come to sell you a dream. Rather, I have come to reveal to you a reality. I believe it is about time we embrace faith in our schools, workplaces, and societies in lieu of ostracizing those who are unashamed to proclaim their faith in the midst of skeptics. Personally, I honor the atheist who is bold about his beliefs more than the alleged Christian whose Christianity only extends to his Facebook religious views. Remember, faith without works is dead.

> For just as the body without the spirit is dead,
> so also faith without works is dead.
> **James 2:26**

Chapter 8

HOLINESS

During senior year, my Thursday evenings were solely devoted to Xcel, a young adults fellowship led by the youth pastor of my home church in Rhode Island, New Life Worship Center. One evening, Pastor Marco advertised that he would be sharing one of his numerous thought-provoking messages that promised to unpack revelation. During the course of his sermon I noticed the content of his oration began to steer towards the topic of Christian holiness. I cringed.

"This is false advertising", I thought to myself.

Historically, I always recoiled when the subject of holiness arose. Even though I had committed myself to the will and ways of God, my mind had retired the archaic doctrine of godliness and holiness with the false premise that the Old Testament had been abolished. For this reason, upon the mention of holiness in the context of mere men, I would establish a hedge around my heart such that the words purely went through one ear, and escaped via the other. As far as I was concerned, only God was holy and men ought not to dare claim holiness as an attribute of a Christian.

As you can imagine, my judgment was desperately flawed. Nonetheless, I believe I am not alone in my misperception of holiness. In fact, it is with much confidence that I make the assertion that many readers probably switched off upon reading the title of this chapter. I find it a great misfortune that a large number of believers in the body of Christ lack understanding in the biblical principle of holiness.

Pastor Marco's unprecedented message on this subject planted the seed in my heart to exhume the truth concerning holiness. If godliness was actually expected of man from God, then it was critical that my ignorance regarding such matters was eliminated. Later that evening, I cried out to God with a sincere heart and a humble spirit, imploring Him to reveal the mystery of holiness to His bondservant.

The following teaching reveals the faithfulness of God in answering the prayers of His children. Be mindful however, that this teaching is not exhaustive of the subject of Christian holiness. The aim of this chapter is merely to cultivate an appreciation for the biblical view on the topic, and perhaps to attack the misconceptions thereof. For a comprehensive teaching, if you so desire to delve deeper, I recommend a book authored by Francis Agyin-Asare entitled: *Upon Delilah's Knees: A Serious Call to Christian Holiness.*

Selective Belief

In the few years I have spent in ministry, it has come to my notice that Christians of our generation possess the scarring trait of selective belief. A large number of people who identify themselves as Christ followers often pick and choose the parts of the Bible that sound appealing, whereas the sour scriptures that are difficult to swallow are treated as meaningless.

In the course of teaching on this subject, I asked the attendees of our Bryant University fellowship this simple question: "by a show of hands, who here believes that they are a child of God?"

Predictably, all hands were eagerly raised and with great pride. And then, I proceeded to enquire as to why they believed that God viewed them as His children. The obvious answer to that was "because the Bible says so".

"Interesting", I thought wittingly, with the knowledge that I had cornered them as I had planned.

The follow up question consequently was this: "by a show of hands, who here believes that they are holy?"

Crickets.

Not a single hand was in the air.

I found this duality fascinating. These Christians believed that they were children of God by virtue of the scriptures, yet did not believe that they were holy even though the same Bible they referenced makes claim of the holiness of the believer.

> But you are a chosen race, a royal priesthood, a holy nation,
> a people for God's own possession, so that you may proclaim

the excellencies of Him who has called you out of
darkness into His marvelous light.

1 Peter 2:9

Why do we choose to believe one and not the other?

There are numerous reasons why selective belief exists in the church today. In the context of holiness, we can legitimately center on two reasons. The first is simply the lack of understanding of New Testament doctrine which will be tacked shortly. Secondly, the public admittance that we are holy calls for accountability—a burden all men tend to reject. In other words, if we call ourselves holy before men, then we would be expected to live up to it daily. In fear of this religious and societal pressure, it appears less appealing to crown ourselves as holy people as the scripture above declares.

Imputed Righteousness

Righteousness is inherited. The death of Christ on the cross effectuated the rightness of the believer before God and hence, a man cannot grow in righteousness. The Bible claims that we are now hidden in Christ and as a result, when God fixes His eyes upon the believer, He sees Christ His beloved Son, who is the manifestation of righteousness.

. . . even the righteousness of God through faith in Jesus
Christ for all those who believe

Romans 3:22

This verse confirms that the righteousness of the Christian comes through belief in the Lord Jesus Christ and is thus inherited. In this vein, there is nothing we can do to become more righteous. The believer can only increase in his revelation of the inherited righteousness:

For in it [the gospel] the righteousness of God is *revealed*
from faith to faith; as it is written, "But the righteous
man shall live by faith."

Romans 1:17

Our revelation of the righteousness inherited is elevated as we increase in faith. This passage of scripture is consistent with the doctrine that the righteousness of God is complete and has been gifted to man by virtue of the sacrifice paid by Jesus Christ our Lord. As we poise ourselves to grow in faith, we are graced to become progressively aware of the righteousness that has been imputed into our spirit man.

Likewise holiness, the concept of being set apart for the will of God, is also inherited. I lay this claim for two reasons, purely based on biblical doctrine. First of all, when man becomes a believer, or a born-again Christian, the Bible helps us to understand that we are now born of the Spirit:

> Jesus answered, "Truly, truly, I say to you, unless one is born
> of water and the Spirit he cannot enter into the kingdom of
> God. That which is born of the flesh is flesh, and that which
> is born of the Spirit is spirit. Do not be amazed that I said to
> you, 'You must be born again'.
>
> **John 3:5-7**

Essentially, Jesus' teaching prescribes that a believer is now born of the Spirit of God, the *Holy* Spirit. Therefore, once we have been born of a holy being, how can we be any different? The principle of reproduction purely from a biological perspective grants that a living thing births posterity after its own kind. The same is true in the realm of the spirit.

The image of God that was lost in mankind in the Garden of Eden was restored in the death and resurrection of Jesus Christ to any man that believes. Now that we have been born of the Holy Spirit, the nature of the Spirit of God has been infused into the genealogy of the first born among many brethren, Jesus Christ. As members of His pedigree, we have now inherited the holiness of the Spirit.

Furthermore, the Spirit of holiness is a gift. It is biblically sound to proclaim that the Holy Spirit is an inheritance from the Father to the believer. Folks, our Christian walk is incomplete until we go past salvation and take hold of our inheritance.

It would surprise you to learn that Jesus was not merely concerned about having our sins forgiven before the Father. If it was so, His resurrection would have been unnecessary as the death of Christ would have sufficed. Perhaps some scriptural basis is in order here:

> And according to the Law, one may almost say,
> all things are cleansed with blood, and without
> shedding of blood there is no forgiveness.
>
> **Hebrews 9:22**

According to the Law of old, the shedding of Christ's blood was sufficient in the remission of the sins of mankind. However, it is intriguing to know that Christ did not stop at death. He resurrected with power on the third day for a reason—that we may receive resurrection power, eternal life, and the inheritance of His Spirit.

Consider this analogy. When a father has an inheritance for his children, say a piece of land, he usually records this inheritance in his will and leaves it with an executor. However, the inheritance in the will is not claimable until the death of the father. As a result, the will is null and void unless the father passes away. The same is true with God the Father.

In eternity past, the Father had an inheritance for His children which was then recorded in His will, now referred to as the Word of God, and left in the hands of the executor, Christ Jesus. This inheritance was the Spirit of God. But until Christ had died, acting on behalf of the Father as the testator, the inheritance could not be attained by His children. For this reason Jesus Christ, who is the visible image of the invisible God, said:

> But I tell you the truth, it is to your advantage that I go away;
> for if I do not go away, the Helper will not come to you;
> but if I go, I will send Him to you.
>
> **John 16:7**

Jesus Christ had to die and resurrect in order for the inheritance of the Spirit to be released to the children of God. Hence, Christ executed the will of God and released the Holy Spirit to believers. Consequently, Christians now have an indwelling holiness as per the inheritance of the Father.

A quote from the great revivalist, Leonard Ravenhill echoes the principle of holiness:

"The wonder of the grace of God is that God can take an unholy man out of an unholy world, make that man holy, and put him back into an unholy world and keep him holy!"

Squandered Inheritance

In the modern church, we have limited the arrival of the Holy Spirit to the works of power and miracles. If I may speak freely, this is the poorest understanding of the primary purpose of the Spirit of God. The scripture below records Christ's instruction to His disciples concerning the Holy Spirit:

> But you will receive power when the Holy Spirit has come
> upon you; and you shall *be* My witnesses both in Jerusalem,

and in all Judea and Samaria, and even to the
remotest part of the earth
Acts 1:8

This verse is often read as an encouragement to witness to the lost. I admit, this is a fair interpretation of this scripture, but it is not the optimal understanding. Jesus Christ in this order does not say the believer will receive power to witness. On the contrary, He declares that the Holy Spirit will infuse power in the believer to *be* a witness. The power of the Spirit is a transformative power not limited to acts, but extends to the very being and nature of man. In essence, Christ alludes to the notion that when the Spirit is received the very nature of the witness conforms to the likeness of the Person whom they are witnessing about. The inheritance of the Spirit is an inheritance of being—holiness is imparted and the nature of man is restored.

Therefore if anyone is in Christ, he is a new creature . . .
2 Corinthians 5:17

The inheritance of holiness has been squandered by virtue of the fact that believers are not alive to the reality that we have already been made holy through the works of the Holy Spirit. The church continues to succumb to sin because many believers are devoid of this understanding.

I brought you into the fruitful land to eat its fruit and
its good things. But you came and defiled My land,
and My inheritance you made an abomination.
Jeremiah 2:7

The Power of the Mind

Holiness begins in the mind. If you do not subscribe to the idea that you are holy, then indeed you will never exhibit the holiness of God. Well hold on, this sounds contradictory. If holiness was inherited, how can we never be holy? The rationale behind this statement is the following. Although holiness was inherited at the point of salvation, God still commands His children to be holy:

Because it is written, "you shall be holy, for I am holy."
1 Peter 1:16

The reason God commands believers to be holy is because He has already equipped us in the being and exhibition of holiness, and as such possesses the right to hold us accountable to it. You see, God commands us to be holy solely because He has made us holy.

A pig does not give birth to a snake—the offspring of a pig is a piglet and snorting is an inherited nature. However, when the piglet is born, it must conform to the nature of the pig—a piglet that comes out hissing is an epic fail. Inherently, the animal is a pig and thus it must act like one.

Likewise, we who have been made holy by the workings of the Holy Spirit must conform to the holiness imputed in us. This was the appeal of the Apostle Paul whilst in bondage for the sake of the Gospel:

> Therefore I, the prisoner of the Lord, implore you to
> walk in a manner worthy of the calling with which
> you have been called.
> **Ephesians 4:1**

As witnesses of Jesus Christ on earth, we have thus been called to holiness and must walk in a manner worthy of that calling. The simplest way to walk in this manner is by internalizing the fact that indeed we have been made holy. When an idea is engrained in your mind, the burden is easier to fulfill. Take our humanity as an example. I doubt any reader of this book woke up in the morning and made a conscious effort to act like a human being. It comes naturally due to the fact that your mind is conditioned to the reality that you are human and as such you must conform to that nature daily. Equally, we must internalize the fact that we are holy, and acts of holiness will come easy. The reason that we often perceive it as difficult to live holy lives on a daily basis is because we regard ourselves as sinful beings—many Christians today continue to live a defeated life in the Law of the Old Testament. It is all in the mind.

The condition of the mind dictates the behavior of man. You see, when a biologically born male with the genitalia to prove it convinces himself that he was meant to be a woman, he gradually takes interest in female affairs, and possibly considers a change in sexual orientation. It started in the mind!

When you begin to internalize the fact that you are holy, your behavior will follow suit! Tithing doesn't make you holy; you are holy so you tithe. Honesty doesn't make you holy; you are holy so you are truthful. Church attendance does not make you holy; you are holy so you attend church. The order of holiness must be grasped.

The Apostle Paul appears to agree to the role of the mind in tackling the issue of holiness:

> Even so *consider* yourselves to be dead to sin,
> but alive to God in Christ Jesus
>
> **Romans 6:11**

Here, Paul trusts that men ought to consider themselves dead to sin. The Apostle's careful choice of diction is riveting. The word 'consider' implies that Christians must convince themselves in their mind that they are no longer slaves to sin. He uses the word 'dead' to connote the fact that men and women of faith must believe that they are unresponsive to the stimulus of temptation.

Holiness is a state of the mind. Once we believe it and internalize it, we will live it. We have been made holy by the power of the Holy Spirit. Be holy!

Chapter 9

THE REST OF THE STORY

Truly, my four years thus far walking with the Lord has been remarkable. From the point of salvation to the journey of maturity, God has sustained me in His work, and I can testify that as promised, all other things have been added unto me.

After successfully completing my senior year, I graduated from Bryant University with magna cum laude honors and a full-time offer with an investment bank in London. I currently reside in the United Kingdom although still in service to the Kingdom of God across borders, in the United States, United Kingdom, and Ghana.

I consider it a pure blessing when I share my testimony with others and they respond in astonishment saying, "wait, how old are you again?" Indeed:

> But God has chosen the foolish things of the world to shame
> the wise, and God has chosen the weak things of the
> world to shame the things which are strong
> **1 Corinthians 1:27**

This chapter is not meant to serve as a closing to the book. In reality, I believe and pray that it symbolizes the introduction of the things yet to come. The words inscribed in this account represent but only a fraction of the entire story. Honestly, when I was instructed to write this book I had no idea what the book was meant to be about, nor did I have a clue whom the intended reader was. But here I sit, by some means, and by some authority, writing words that I could have never imagined I would even speak.

A good eye will notice that I have presented a narrative from the early years of my life until the very moment I am sitting down writing this book. Funny, I do not even know how I am going to bring it to a conclusion. But I don't need to. Only God knows the end from the beginning, the Author and the Finisher of our faith.

God bless you.

Message to the Reader

If you have been blessed by this book, I strongly encourage you to recommend it to a friend. We are blessed to be a blessing unto others; hence it is only noble to pass this on to those in your circle of influence. Furthermore, I openly welcome your thoughts and feedback on this piece—please send all comments to the address below if private, otherwise all public remarks would be preferred on the Facebook page.

Thank you for being a blessing.

Mail: crossroads.bk@gmail.com
Facebook: facebook.com/crossroads.bk

Lightning Source UK Ltd.
Milton Keynes UK
UKOW050156280712

196700UK00002B/14/P